You are Unique

Written by Suzanne Tonner Okerfelt

Illustrated by Brad Tonner

This book is dedicated to
all the children who
have touched my heart!

You are
Unique

Written by Suzanne Tonner Okerfelt

Illustrated by Brad Tonner

Published by The Road Less Traveled Press

The teacher sat in a circle with her students quite unique.
She looked around at all of them and then began to speak.
"Does anyone have something to share?
Does anyone have a question?"

This is how she started each and every session.

Their hands were waving in the air and some began to speak!
"Everyone will have a chance. Let's begin with Jill, then Pete."

"What are special needs?" Pete said to her, looking kind of lonely.
"It means that you are different,"
Jill chimed in. "It means you don't fit in."

"You are unique!" the teacher said " I am very glad you are."
The room got quiet. There was no sound as everyone just gazed!
The teacher then began to speak to them in her own special way.
She explained their gifts, their special ways and soon
"unique" was fun!

She spoke to every child she had, unique, each and everyone.

"You are the only one with glasses"
she said as she looked at little Mike.
"You never miss a single thing. With glasses
you have perfect sight!"

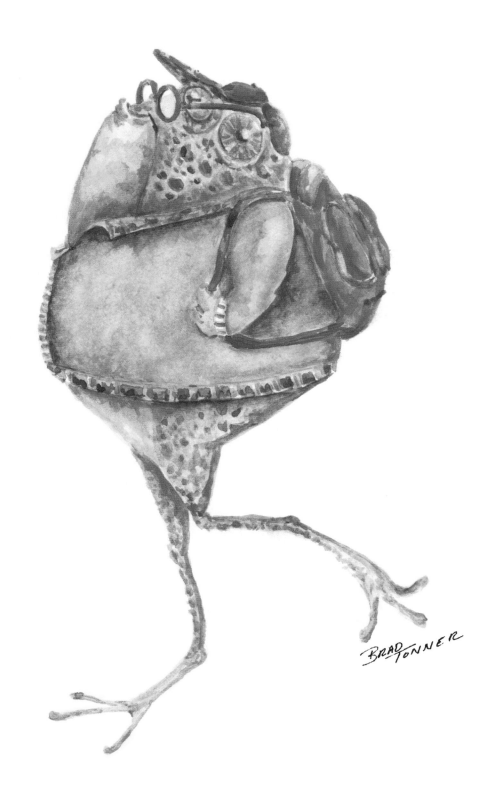

"You sing in the chorus. You are best at games.
If you do not feel special,
it really is a shame."

"You are the only one with a wheelchair,"
she said to little Joe.
"You fly quickly through the halls,
faster than anyone I know."

"You are on the student council
and you have so many friends.
We look to you for help with things.
On you we all depend."

"You are unique," she said to Matt who sat off by himself.
"You see the world as no else and sometimes that is hard.
But, when people understand how you think,
they know you will go far!"

11

"Your paintings they are beautiful, your colors
are bright and fun.
Everyone wants you to draw and share
your art with everyone!"

Little Kelly sat quite still she wasn't sure you see.
Her health made it hard to play,
but it was nothing you could see.

15

The teacher smiled at Kelly "You are unique as well.
You deal with sickness everyday but no one else can tell.
You clap for others, you cheer them on and wish that you
could play. When it comes to friendship,
you always save the day!"

"Your brain makes reading difficult,"
she said to little Lou.
You hate the letters d and b because
they turn the word around.
It isn't easy for you to read as others
seem to do, but it will
never stop you from being
successful, too!"

"You are on the student council.
You are the best at softball too.
You can jump higher than
anyone else can do."

"Your hands have trouble writing,"
she said to little Jen.
Others look at what you write and
think you do not know how to use a pen.
But when you keyboard
or we scribe your ideas just glow.
Then the people all around
find out what you really know."

24

"When your school work is finished
and you begin to do ballet,
you twirl and spin so beautifully
you take my breath away!"

Ben sat there quietly, a little shy to talk,
he often had some trouble when he began to speak.
He worried that someone would laugh or
maybe they would tease, yet when it came to
music he was the best you see.

27

When he plays his clarinet
and marches in with the band
everyone begins to cheer for him.
They are his biggest fans.

Mike sat in the middle.
He was neither loud nor strong.
He stayed inside his shell
afraid his answer might be wrong.
He was so shy and quiet it made
it hard to know him well.

31

But when there is something broken especially a car,
he is a great mechanic the very best by far.

You fit right in to every day just like everyone you see,
who starts each and every day just like you hoping
for something fun and new in each and every way.

You are unique and I am glad that you are who you are.
I admire everyone of you, you all have come so far.

You are unique and wonderful, no matter who you are.

You are unique and wonderful,
Like each and every star!

Made in the USA
Charleston, SC
11 September 2013